EXCITING TITLES FROM Scholastic EDUCATION

Contemporary Fiction & Sports Adventures

TALES OF THE UNCOOL
6-Book Series

These are the stories of the nerds, geeks, and freaks of Halsey Middle School — and how six self-proclaimed 'uncool' tweens took over their school.

Grades: 4-6
Ages: 8-12   Paperbacks: $8.99
Pages: 64   Library Bound: $27.99

MAGIC LOCKER ADVENTURES
6-Book Series

Three young friends find a magic locker, which takes them back in time. Historic sporting events are in jeopardy unless they right history!

Grades: 3-5
Ages: 8-11   Paperbacks: $8.99
Pages: 48   Library Bound: $27.99

ON THE HARDWOOD 30-Book Series

MVP Books invites readers to stand alongside their favorite NBA superstars *On the Hardwood*. These officially licensed NBA team bios provide an exciting opportunity to learn about where a team has been, and where they are going...

Grades: 4-6
Ages: 8-12   Paperbacks: $8.99
Pages: 48   Library Bound: $27.99

Common Core Aligned   twitter.com/bookbuddymedia   facebook.com/bookbuddymedia

ORDER NOW!

Contact Lerner Publisher Services:
www.LernerBooks.com
Call: 800-328-4929 • **Fax:** 800-332-1132

Lerner
PUBLISHER SERVICES

BOSTON MARATHON

BY JUSTIN PETERSEN

World's Greatest Sporting Events: Boston Marathon

Scobre Educational
2255 Calle Clara
La Jolla, CA 92037

Scobre Operations & Administration
42982 Osgood Road
Fremont, CA 94539

www.scobre.com
info@scobre.com

Scobre Educational publications may be purchased for
educational, business, or sales promotional use.

Cover and layout design by Jana Ramsay
Edited by Zach Wyner
Copyedited by Renae Reed
Some photos by Newscom

ISBN: 978-1-62920-158-0 (Soft Cover)
ISBN: 978-1-62920-157-3 (Library Bound)
ISBN: 978-1-62920-156-6 (eBook)

INDEX

INTRODUCTION

Every third Monday in April, the people of Massachusetts take to the streets to celebrate **Patriots' Day**. The Boston Red Sox play an early baseball game, beginning at 11 a.m., while hundreds of thousands of fans amass along the storied 26.2-mile route of the Boston **Marathon**. As the Red Sox game ends and fans spill out of Fenway Park, they squeeze themselves into every available space on the bleacher-lined sidewalks. Marathon runners enter the homestretch and Kenmore Square rumbles with applause, creating an atmosphere and a tradition unlike any other in American sports. In 2014, this tradition meant more to the people of Boston than ever before.

In 2013, two brothers conspired to bring violence and mayhem to Boston. They placed a pair of bombs near the finish line and detonated them during the race, killing three people and injuring 300 more. The act was one of cruelty and hatred. It was meant to injure not only innocent bystanders, but also to curb the excitement, joy and wonder inspired by this great event. However, if the 2014 Boston Marathon demonstrated

A memorial for victims of the 2013 Boston Marathon bombing.

anything, it was that violence does not generate the desired result. The tragic events of Patriots' Day 2013 gave rise to the popular expression "Boston Strong." One year later, the people of Boston demonstrated their strength.

On April 21, 2014, nearly 36,000 people donned shorts, **tank tops** and **cross trainers** and competed in the Boston Marathon—the most since the race's 100-year anniversary in 1996. Many of these participants had been at the race the previous year; some of them had been severely injured. In addition to the high number of participants, half a million spectators came out to watch the event, showing that they could not be scared away. These resilient racing fans cheered their hearts out as three-time Olympian Meb Keflezighi became the race's first American winner in 30 years.

36,000 runners turned out to make the 2014 Boston Marathon one of the largest in history.

A LOOK BACK

As supporters of Meb Keflezighi cheered him down the homestretch of the 2014 Boston Marathon, they chanted "Boston Strong! Meb Strong!" Keflezighi crossed the finish line with a time of 2:08:37, becoming the first American to win the race in three decades. He said that he wanted to honor the victims of the 2013 tragedy. While he certainly accomplished this goal, so did every one of the half a million people who came out on Patriots' Day 2014 to participate in this great tradition—a tradition that began 118 years earlier under much more modest circumstances.

To say that the Boston Marathon has increased in popularity over the years would be the understatement of the century. The history of the modern marathon dates

back to 1896 and the first modern Olympic Games. At those games, a man named Michel Bréal sparked interest in establishing a marathon to honor the long-distance running competitions held in ancient Greece. The event was a success. A year later, the idea of holding a marathon migrated to Boston, Massachusetts.

The ancient Olympic Philippeion in Olympia, Greece, site of the ancient Olympic Games.

The Boston Marathon begins in Hopkinton, Massachusetts.

In 1897, the **Boston Athletic Association (B.A.A.)** created the road race that would gain a reputation as one of the most challenging marathons in the world. Eighteen runners participated in Boston's first grueling 24.5-mile run. John McDermott–the winner of the first American marathon held in New York in 1896–took the lead during the hard hills of Newton and held on to win with a time of just less than three hours. Eight runners had bowed out due to **exhaustion** or injury; McDermott was one of only 10 men to complete the race.

The difficult race ends at the intersection of Boylston and Dartmouth.

Following its first year, the race steadily grew in popularity. By 1902, five years after the race's beginning, the number of runners increased from 18 to 49. These runners seemed better prepared for the difficult trek, with 42 of them finishing the race. Among them was a 16-year-old high-school student named Charlie Moody, who came in fourth with a time of 3:28:47. It was a remarkable feat that would not be possible under today's standards, as runners must now be 18 years old to qualify.

In the early 20th century, the Boston Marathon grew into an **international event**, with runners flocking to Boston from Canada, Finland and Germany. These competitors came from all walks of life—from Olympic athletes to busboys. Whatever their background, they sought the same thing—the unique physical and mental challenges of long-distance running. The number of runners fell during World War I and World War II, but the race continued. By the late 1960s, the number of annual participants swelled into the thousands.

In some ways, the growth of the Boston Marathon mirrors the growth of the country. While the race has been harmed by incidents that were embarrassing and shameful, it has also been the site of great courage, triumph and social change. One source of shame was the race's history of **sexism**. Incredibly, women were not allowed to compete in the race for nearly 70 years. It wasn't until 1966 that Roberta "Bobbi" Gibb became the first woman ever to complete the race, and she did so unofficially, without a **bib** number. A year later, Kathrine Switzer became the first woman ever to race and finish with a bib number. She completed the race despite an ugly incident in which an official attempted to tear her number from her sweatshirt. Because of brave women like Gibb and Switzer, the B.A.A. decided to officially allow women to participate in 1972. Today, women comprise nearly half of the racing field.

Kathrine Switzer has dedicated her career to creating better opportunities for women everywhere.

The Boston Marathon proudly welcomes disabled athletes.

These days, the giant field of Boston Marathon participants excludes no one. It includes people of all races, creeds and colors, from all across the gender spectrum. It also includes the handicapped. In 2014, many handicapped participants—some of whom had been severely injured in the 2013 bombings—demonstrated the heart and resolve that has made this marathon one of the most enduring sporting events in the world.

Fans line the streets and extend their hands
to racers for an occasional high-five.

TIMELINE

1947
Suh Yun-bok sets the men's world record at 2:25:39. He is the first Asian champion and, at a height of five-feet, one-inch, the smallest winner in Boston Marathon history.

1890 — 1920 — 1950 — 1980

1897
After witnessing the positive reaction to the marathon race in the previous year's Olympic Games, the B.A.A. establishes its own race. Eighteen runners compete in the first-ever Boston Marathon.

1924
The length of the race is modified for the first and last time. To mimic a true Olympic marathon, runners are required to complete 26.2 miles.

1967
Kathrine Switzer registers as K. Switzer and becomes the first registered female participant. When a racing official attempts to physically eject her from the race, Switzer's boyfriend barrels into the official, knocking him off the road.

1918
World War I puts a stop to the marathon for one year. In its place, military personnel participate in a relay race made of 10-man teams. Camp Devens of Ayer, Massachusetts takes home the title.

1986
For the first time in the history of the event, the winner receives a cash prize. Australia's Rob de Castella sets a course record of 2:07:51. He receives a $25,000 prize, a $5,000 performance bonus and a new car.

1996
In the race's 100th year, it sets a world record for the largest marathon with 36,748 starters and 35,868 finishers.

2014
Meb Keflezighi dedicates his run to the victims of the bombings, and with a time of 2:08:37, becomes the first American winner in 30 years. Despite the previous year's bombings, the race boasts 36,00 participants and half a million spectators.

2011
Kenyan runner Geoffrey Mutai runs the fastest marathon ever, finishing with a time of 2:03:02.

2000   **2005**   **2010**   **2015**

2004
With the number of participants in the tens of thousands, officials vary the start times so the streets will not be too congested.

2013
Tragedy strikes as two bombs explode near the finish line, killing three people and injuring several hundred others. The remaining runners receive finishing medals, despite the fact that they cannot complete the course.

THE FUTURE

With more than a century of racing under its belt, the B.A.A. can rest easy, knowing that it has seen just about everything. The Boston Marathon has endured discrimination, war and terrorism en route to becoming an essential part of the local and national culture. In a city stuffed to the gills with history, this race adds remarkable tales of determination, grit and heroism with each passing year.

Equipment

Many sports require athletes to spend vast sums of money on the latest and most technologically advanced gear. Without it, athletes run the risk of falling behind the pack. While the athletes who compete in the Boston Marathon are no different, thankfully, the equipment required is minimal.

Long-distance running is a solo sport. Runners only need to focus on a few important items–the most important of which is the running shoe.

Running on asphalt and concrete for 26.2 miles is tough on a runner's feet. Running shoes must cushion athletes' feet from the repetitive pounding so they don't become too sore to continue. A good shoe also protects other parts of the body, such as knees and shins, which can become sources of intense pain if not properly cared for.

The right type of clothing is also necessary, both for training as well as racing. Weather is an especially important consideration when purchasing **performance clothes**. Runners must be prepared to perform rain or shine. Performance tank tops and shorts are a must-have for the warmer days. Winter gear consists of performance running pants and jackets, designed to block harsh winds while still allowing the skin to breathe.

German runner Uta Pippig crosses the finish line to win the women's division of the 100th Boston Marathon.

VENUE

A view of the Boston skyline as seen from the Boston Harbor.

Beginning in Hopkinton, Massachusetts, the legendary course for the Boston Marathon winds its way through eight towns and cities before ending in downtown Boston. Most of these towns and cities have participated in the race from the beginning. The town of Hopkinton became the starting point in 1924 when the course was lengthened from 24.5 to 26.2 miles.

Set-up for the race includes **grandstands** in Hopkinton and Kenmore Square, as well as several critical stations. The most important of these are the **hydration stations**. From Mile 2 to Mile 25, these stations provide runners the opportunity to replenish their bodies with sports drinks and water. Volunteers line the entirety of Mile 17, wearing colored shirts that indicate the PowerBar flavor they are passing out. Runners in need of calories to convert to energy gratefully accept these offerings and then literally eat and run.

Runners pass by a water station and thousands of discarded cups lay as proof.

In addition to these fuel stations, some runners require a different kind of pit stop. To see to it that these needs are met, restrooms are also available throughout the race at marked spots.

RULES

The Boston Marathon is all-inclusive, meaning that anyone can join in the race. However, the registered runners that compete for the title are the best of the best. None of them step up to the starting line without first proving that they deserve to be there. Qualifying times, determined by the B.A.A., vary according to age and whether or not a person is physically handicapped.

Amongst participants, 18- to 34-year-olds make up the largest age group in the race. Men in this group can qualify with a time of three hours and five minutes or less, while women must have a time at or less than three hours and 35 minutes. In order to meet these expectations, racers must compete in what is called a "feeder" race. Such races are run throughout the year–the B.A.A. has a long list of acceptable feeder races.

14,343 women finished the 2014 Boston Marathon, approximately 98 percent of the female runners that started the race.

Some runners have a more lighthearted approach to the running of the race.

The 2013 Boston Marathon resulted in some rule changes in order to enhance security. Backpacks, strollers and costumes that cover faces are not allowed in the Athletes' Village, at the start area or finish line. Sadly, rules concerning "**Bandits**" (people who join the race without registering) have been modified, discouraging a time-honored tradition that was tolerated for many years.

THE ROAD TO...

Running a marathon is incredibly difficult and can't be accomplished without months of difficult training. This doesn't stop tens of thousands of ordinary people from devoting countless hours, and sacrificing months' worth of dessert, as they chase their goal of running in the Boston Marathon.

The first step toward the completion of a marathon is the training plan. Race training has to be done safely, with a gradual increase in the number of miles attempted and a lot of rest in between runs. A common mistake that many young runners make is not allowing enough time for their bodies to recover. Rest allows runners to dig deep without constantly overusing their muscles and increasing their risk of injury. Anticipating race conditions, running in different kinds of weather and incorporating elements of the course are all critical parts of the training.

Programs for training the body for a marathon run can be completed at the beginner, intermediate and advanced levels, each with the goal of elevating a runner to the next level of racing. Runners are encouraged to stretch and build their muscles with some light

Stretching is required if runners hope to avoid injury during rigorous training.

Every marathon runner that breaks the finish-line tape has followed a strict training regimen.

weight lifting so that smaller muscle groups can compensate when major muscles start to become too tired to carry the load.

Becoming a top racer requires practice at a marathon pace. This means that part of the training requires runners to run at the speed planned for the big race day. Runners that meet their goal time in training are far more likely to attain it when the big day finally arrives.

BEST PERFORMANCES

GEOFFREY KIPRONO MUTAI, 2011

Geoffrey Kiprono Mutai was born in Kenya and began running in 1994. With a win in the 2008 Monaco Marathon, Mutai established himself as one of the best long-distance runners in the world.

The 2011 Boston Marathon provided one of the greatest finishes in the history of long-distance running. Mutai and fellow Kenyan Moses Mosop matched one another stride for stride over the last few miles of the race. Although they had run at a blistering pace, both men refused to succumb to fatigue. Then, in the final mile, Mutai dug deeper and discovered a well of energy. He sprinted toward the finish line, crossing it four seconds ahead of Mosop. For 26.2 miles, Mutai had averaged a incredible pace of four minutes and 42 seconds per mile. He finished the race with a time of 2:03:02, the fastest marathon time ever recorded.

MEB KEFLEZIGHI, 2014

Meb Keflezighi was born in Eritrea and immigrated to the United States at the age of 12. A dominant runner in high school, he won a silver medal at the 2004 Summer Olympic Games and he won the 2009 New York City Marathon.

In 2014, Americans were eager to show that their enjoyment of the great tradition that is the Boston Marathon was not going to be impaired by the tragic bombing of the previous year. While they expected a day of triumph, few anticipated the first American winner in 30 years.

Meb Keflezighi raced the final miles of the 2014 Boston Marathon with Wilson Chebet hot on his heels. As the crowd chanted the words "Boston Strong! Meb Strong!" Meb pulled away from the competition and won the race with a time of 2:08:37. With a huge smile on his face, Meb proclaimed that although he hadn't set a new world record, "I've got the Boston Marathon title."

BOB HALL, 1975

At the age of 24, Bob Hall became the first sanctioned wheelchair participant in Boston Marathon history. In 1975, Bob Hall wrote a letter to Boston Marathon director Will Cloney, asking permission to participate in the race. While Cloney did not allow Hall to officially register and receive a bib number, he said that if Hall was able to complete the race in less than three hours and 30 minutes, he would be recognized as an official finisher.

Racing for the advancement of handicapped people everywhere, Hall crossed the finish line with a time of 2:58:00. His accomplishment led to the creation of the wheelchair division of the race, a division that has attracted more than 1,400 participants since 1975.

RITA JEPTOO, 2014

Rita Jeptoo of Kenya is one of the world's most dominant long-distance runners. She has won two half marathons and six marathons, including three Boston Marathon titles.

In 2014, Rita Jeptoo, winner of the 2006 and 2013 Boston Marathon, fought valiantly to defend her title. Eight years removed from a personal best time of 2:23:38, Jeptoo was motivated by her desire to win in record fashion.

As the 2014 Boston Marathon began, veteran Shalane Flanagan set a blazing early pace. Jeptoo worried about her chances, saying later that, "My body was not feeling well." Gradually, her body began to feel better and Jeptoo gained confidence and strength. After finally grabbing the lead at Heartbreak Hill, one of the hardest parts of the race, she left the pack of skilled runners behind. At Mile 23, she ran a four minute and 48 second mile, her fastest of the day. She went on to win the race and set a new course record with an incredible time of 2:18:57.

THE RECORD BOOK

South Korean Suh Yun-bok crossed the finish line in 1947 with a time of 2:25:39, winning the Boston Marathon in world record time.

Fastest Time, Women's Division: Rita Jeptoo registered a record-setting pace of 2:18:57 in the 2014 Boston Marathon and took home her third career Boston Marathon title.

Fastest Time, Men's Division: In 2011, Geoffrey Mutai set a course record with a time of 2:03:02. He sprinted the final miles to beat fellow Kenyan runner Moses Mosop by four seconds.

Fastest Time, Men's Wheelchair Division: With a London Marathon win already under his belt, Josh Cassidy came into the Boston Marathon race prepared to make waves. He cruised over the finish line with a record-setting time of 1:18:25.

Fastest Time, Women's Wheelchair Division: Wakako Tsuchida, the first wheelchair athlete from Japan, set the course record with a time of 1:34:06. Between 2007 and 2011, she won five consecutive Boston Marathons.

Over the course of his Boston Marathon career, Kenyan runner Robert Kipkoech Cheruiyot has earned the most prize money. With victories in 2003, 2006, 2007 and 2008, Cheruiyot earned $469,000.

THE FANS

Fan-created memorial site for the victims of the 2013 attack.

The Boston Marathon has become one of the most highly attended sporting events in the world. Because the fans can line the streets and interact with the runners, they feel that they are true participants, and as such, they can influence the outcome of the race. Their encouragement can certainly provide exhausted runners a much-needed boost, especially in the race's final agonizing miles. If not for the cheers of "Boston Strong! Meb Strong!" who knows whether or not Meb Keflezighi would have pulled out his 2014 victory.

Fans gather along Boylston Street near the end of the marathon.

With the race winding through eight towns and cities, spectators get the chance to check out the local shops, restaurants and other attractions. This element of exploration and discovery makes attending the Boston Marathon that much more appealing. Thousands of families pile into the car and make a day of it, while thousands more watch the broadcast from home. The 2014 Boston Marathon saw record highs in viewership. From 9 a.m. to 4 p.m., the average attendance was 260,000. As Meb Keflezighi entered the final stretch and headed for the finish line, that number peaked at half a million.

IMPACT

With more than a century of history, the Boston Marathon is one of the oldest sporting events in existence. Taking place on Patriots' Day and coinciding with an early Red Sox game, it is a uniquely spectator-friendly event that attracts one of the largest crowds in all of sports. With those large crowds comes a great deal of attention—for the city, its businesses and its people. This attention helps generate **economic growth**.

Participating in the Boston Marathon is a goal for all runners who aspire to compete at the professional level. And the desire to compete for the Boston Marathon title has spiked in interest in qualifying marathons everywhere. Boston Marathon hopefuls compete in races all over the world with the hope of earning their place on the starting line in Hopkinton, Massachusetts. Simply donning the coveted bib number is an achievement all its own. It distinguishes a runner as a participant in a community of dedicated long-distance runners and establishes them as competitors on one of sports' oldest and most storied stages.

The Boston Marathon finish line on Boylston Street.

GLOSSARY

bandit: a person who participates in the race without registering.

bib: a piece of cloth or plastic bearing a number, usually worn over the chest or back, identifying a competitor in a race.

Boston Athletic Association (B.A.A.): a non-profit, organized sports association for the city of Boston, Massachusetts. It hosts such events as the world-renowned Boston Marathon.

cross trainers: a type of athletic shoe designed to be used in more than one type of activity.

economic growth: an increase in the amount of goods and services produced per person over a period of time.

exhaustion: a state of extreme tiredness.

grandstand: the main seating area, usually roofed, commanding the best view for spectators at racetracks or sports stadiums.

Heartbreak Hill: an ascent over 0.4 mile between the 20- and 21-mile marks, near Boston College.

hydration station: an area designated for the distribution of water and other hydrating fluids.

international event: an event involving participants from various nations.

marathon: a long-distance running race, strictly one of 26 miles and 385 yards.

Patriots' Day: a civic holiday commemorating the anniversary of the Battles of Lexington and Concord on April 19, 1775. These were the first battles of the American Revolutionary War.

performance clothes: clothing that performs or functions for some purpose. Performance clothing helps athletes and active people keep cool, comfortable and dry through moisture management and other techniques.

sexism: prejudice, stereotyping or discrimination, typically against women, on the basis of sex.

tank top: a close-fitting sleeveless top.